Hammerhead Shark

Curious Kids Press

Hammerhead Shark

The Hammerhead Shark is a very odd and a very cool undersea creature. This shark is just one of over 470 different species of sharks living in the oceans today. This fish is closely related to the ray. There are 9 species of the Hammerhead Shark. These are just some of the fun facts about the Hammerhead Shark. So sit back and be prepared to sink your teeth into more interesting things about this toothy creature.

Where in the World?

Did you know the Hammerhead Shark will live in both shallow and deep water? They like warm and kind of warm water. In fact, in the summertime (when the water gets too warm) they will migrate in large numbers to find cooler water. These sharks can be found as far down as 260 feet (80 meters) below the ocean surface.

The Body of the Hammerhead Shark

Did you know the Hammerhead Shark has a weird head? Just like its name, the Hammerhead Shark has a head shaped like a hammer. Its small eyes are on the ends of its hammer-head. This shark also has a tall dorsal fin. This is the one that sticks out of the water.

The Size of a Hammerhead Shark

Did you know the Hammerhead Shark can grow to be very large? The average size of the Hammerhead Shark is 11.5 feet long (3.5 meters). It can weigh around 500 pounds (230 kilograms). Despite its size, most of the Hammerheads are harmless to people. Except one. We will learn about that one later on.

The Skin of the Hammerhead Shark

Did you know the skin of the Hammerhead Shark is very tough? Unlike some sea creatures, the Hammerhead Shark has a thick cartilage. This is like the end of your nose. The Hammerhead Shark is gray-brown in color on top. Its belly is an off-white color. This color-combo helps it stay hidden when it hunts.

The Senses of the Hammerhead Shark

Did you know the Hammerhead's wide-set eyes help it locate food? As we already learned, this shark has its eyes on the ends of its hammer-head. Its eyes can see in many directions and are better than some other sharks. The Hammerhead also has special sensors on its head. These let the shark feel when there is prey close by.

The Teeth of a Hammerhead Shark

Did you know the mouth of the Hammerhead may be smaller, but it still has sharp teeth? This type of shark has two rows of teeth on both its jaws. Its teeth are triangular in shape and very sharp. They also have a serrated edge to them, like a saw.

What the Hammerhead Shark Eats

Did you know the Hammerhead Shark is a carnivore? This means this shark only likes to eat meat. It will dine on fish, squid, crabs, lobsters and other sea creatures. But its favorite food has got to be the stingray. Even though the stingray can be deadly, the Hammerhead has a special way to hunt it.

How the Hammerhead Shark Hunts

Did you know the Hammerhead Shark hunts the stingray using its head? When a Hammerhead spots a stingray it will quickly approach it. The Hammerhead will grab the ray then hold it down with its hammer-like head. The hungry shark will then chomp down on the rays wings to keep it from fleeing.

Enemies of the Hammerhead Shark

Did you know the Hammerhead Shark only has 2 enemies? The first enemy to the Hammerhead is man. This fish is caught and used for its fins. The second enemy to this shark is other Hammerhead Sharks. When really hungry, the Hammerhead will eat smaller Hammerhead Sharks.

The Hammerhead Shark Mom

Did you know the mother Hammerhead feeds her young when they are inside of her? The mom Hammerhead has her babies inside of her body. She can carry from 12 to 15 baby sharks at once. After the mother Hammerhead gives birth, she swims away and leaves the babies on their own.

Baby Hammerheads

Did you know the baby Hammerheads are called, pups? The pups are born fully developed. Once they are born they swim away from their mother. However, the young will stay huddled together until they grow and develop more. The heads of the Hammerhead pups are more rounded than hammer-like.

Life of the Hammerhead Shark

Did you know the Hammerhead Shark can live to be quite old? In nature a Hammerhead Shark can live from 20 to 30 years. Most species of this shark are very peaceful and just want to be left alone.   Attacks on people are rare. However, there are a few Hammerheads that are very mean. Read on...

The Great Hammerhead Shark

Did you know this is the biggest Hammerhead Shark species? This Hammerhead is not only the biggest, it is the meanest. It can measure about 13 feet long (4 meters) and weigh about 500 pounds (227 kilograms). It is very aggressive and will attack. It can be found in most of the warm water oceans.

The Bonnethead Shark

Did you know this is the smallest of all the Hammerhead species? This species is very shy and timid. It only grows to be about 3 to 5 feet long (0.91 to 1.52 meters). It is gray-brown on top with a white underbelly. Like all Hammerhead Sharks, this one has to keep swimming to avoid sinking to the bottom of the ocean.

Quiz

Question 1: How many species of the Hammerhead are there?

Answer 1: 9 species

Question 2: What will a Hammerhead Shark do when the water gets too warm?

Answer 2: It migrates (or moves) to cooler waters

Question 3: Where are the eyes of this shark located ?

Answer 3: On the ends of its hammer-like head

Question 4: What is the Hammerhead Shark's favorite food?

Answer 4: The Stingray

Question 5: Do the baby sharks live alone or in groups?

Answer 5: They live in small groups until they grow and mature.

Thank you for checking out another title from Curious Kids Press! Make sure to search "Curious Kids Press" on Amazon.com for many other great books.

CPSIA information can be obtained at www.ICGtesting.com
Printed in the USA
BVIW12n2339171215
PP6628900001B/5